SWEET RIVER SONG

Hyacinth E. Hughes

Sweet River Song

Published by:

Sisserou Press
Roseau
Commonwealth of Dominica

The author has represented that she is the sole author of the material written in this publication. The author has further represented and warranted full ownership and/or legal rights to publish all the materials in this book.

All Rights Reserved.

Copyright © 2016 Hyacinth E. Hughes

Illustrations by Canita Ruan.

This book may not be reproduced, transmitted, or stored in whole or in part by any means, including graphic, electronic, or mechanical without the express written consent of the author except in the case of brief quotations embodied in critical articles and reviews.

ISBN: 978-976-95898-0-3

Sisserou Press is an imprint of Emmanuel Publishing House. Sisserou Press and the "SP" logo are trademarks belonging to Emmanuel Publishing House.

www.emmanuelpublishinghouse.com
emmanuelpublications99@gmail.com

Table of Contents

Acknowledgements vi

Preface vii

Dedication ix

Part 1 The Nation

Anguilla, Look Where You Came From 2

My Island Home 4

I weep for you my country 5

Dry Weather 7

Folklore 9

Anguillian Politics 10

Part 2 School Life

The Principal 14

My Students 17

Miss Moore And The Class 17

Memories Of My Primary School Days 20

The Fight 23

Part 3 Life Experiences

Growing Pains 28

A Mother's Care 30

What Does Grandma Mean? 31

Children are God's Gifts 32

Grandmar Can 34

Brother John-The Preacher Man 36

Life's Journey 38

Fighting the Odds 39

What Can You Do? 41

Pass on God's love 43

Give Thanks 44

The Senses 45

A Recipe for Success 47

The Witching Hours 48

Time 50

Sweet River Song 53

The Quest 55

Romeo 57

Confrontation with a Masked Man 58

A Personal Experience of Hurricane Donna 59

If Only 60

Election Fever 62

Jamaican Bus Ride 65

Am I Losing It? 68

Part 4 Limericks

Limericks 74

Acknowledgements

I wish to express deep appreciation and thanks to the organizers of the Malliouhanna Poetry Competition – The Anguilla Public Library and the University Centre which provided the opportunity for me to compete with other established Anguillian writers. This annual competition was the launching pad from which I took off on a voyage of rediscovery into the world of poetry.

I wish to acknowledge the valuable assistance and contributions of the following persons:

Mrs. Rita Celestine-Carty, a language teacher at the Albena Lake-Hodge Comprehensive School who willingly read through my poems, edited them and gave useful suggestions where necessary. Mrs. Susan Sayre for her editorial recommendations and useful suggestions.

My children who became my sounding boards, critics and encouragers, particularly my daughters who would say- "Mom stop saying you are going to publish your poems soon.
Just get it done."

My husband Elvet, who listened patiently to my early attempts, read the poems through and gave his views. I wish to thank him particularly for putting up with the many hours of neglect while I was busily composing my poems at nights, and for encouraging me every step of the way.

Mrs. Candis Niles, Director of Tourism who invited me to participate in the poetry reading sessions at Lit Fest 2013 and 2014. Thanks also for encouraging me to continue to write my poetry and get published.

I also wish to acknowledge the many valuable ideas and inspiration gained from reading a wide selection of language, poetry and story books.

Preface

As a standard bearer goes before the King, so, too, does the poet go before the nation's history, articulating the essence of a people's psyche. Mrs Hyacinth Hughes is one such culture bearer. A lover of the spoken and written word and well steeped in the folklore of Anguilla. For most of her life Mrs Hughes has been intimately involved in the field of education, first as a primary school teacher, moving up the ranks to the positions of Primary School Principal and Education Officer. In the classroom, her passion for writing and performing stories, poems rhymes and songs engaged her students in the learning process, and spilled over into places like the church and the Public Library's literacy programme where cultural traditions could be passed on to the next generation. Mrs Hughes is a regular participant in the Malliouhana Poetry Competition since its inception in 2007 with poems that have always garnered acclaim. In 2012, she emerged as the first place winner.

In 2013, her ultimate dream of writing poetry that would foster that deep love and appreciation which she experienced as a primary school pupil, was reawakened. Inspired by the authors and writers she met at the first Anguilla Lit Fest: 'A Literary Jollification', she vowed to commit to her writing vocation, starting with writing a few lines every day. Just two years later her passion for the spoken and written word has given birth to a collection of poems and limericks which she has entitled '*Sweet River Song*'. To you, Teacher Hyacinth (as she is affectionately known), we say Congratulations, and best wishes on achieving this milestone, a reminder that dreams never die - they lie dormant within us, waiting the maturing showers of encouragement and faith. To you the readers, indeed, the rich repertoire of words from the pen of Hyacinth Hughes will doubtless provoke contemplation, reflection and certainly inspiration.

Candis Niles,
Director of Tourism, Anguilla.

DEDICATION:

To my immediate family, my husband Elvet, and my children Deirdre, Doyle and Deslyn Hughes and to my parents, Viola Richardson and the late Baldwin Richardson.

The Nation

Anguilla, Look Where You Came From

Do you remember when life was hard and things were rough,

With no where to turn and nothing to do?

But your people are resilient, your people are tough

They toiled laboriously just to make it through.

Picking salt, tilling the soil, plowing the seas,

Were the only means of making a living

Mauby bark, livestock and green pigeon peas

Even thatch brooms earned us a shilling.

After years of oppression, struggle and deprivation,

We appealed to central government to improve our lot.

Our cries went unheeded, we made the decision,

To free ourselves from that hated Despot.

We implored Mother England to decide our fate,

Grant us self rule or govern us anew.

"Oh no!" they cried, "You'll be part of a state,

Rule from 'Central' is the best thing for you."

"We want no part of a three-island state!"

This bold band of freedom fighters cried.

Everything stood at stalemate;

Anguillians would no longer be denied.

Talks of statehood still made headway,

So our bold leaders decided to take matters in hand.

May 30th dawned, what a fateful day!

When we expelled their lawmen from our land.

Forty years ago you headlined every front page,

Unknown till then, you emerged from total obscurity

Into a prime tourism destination – a new image:

A land of peace, hope and prosperity.

Anguilla you have come a long way.

Let's honour our stalwart men and women

Who envisioned a brighter future for us today

Let us be united now as we were back then.

My Island Home

In the Caribbean chain there lies a little isle

Where local people greet you with a warm, friendly smile;

An island that's serenaded in poem and in song,

Anguilla, my island, the place where I belong.

Long and narrow is this tiny, tranquil isle,

Yet its natural beauty will enchant you for a while,

You'll certainly enjoy the treasures found here:
Sand, sea, sun- the best you'll ever share.

This beautiful gem surrounded by deep blue sea
Is an island paradise, dear to you and me;
Hordes of tourists come here to unwind
From all the hustle and bustle they leave behind.

I envy none who live in jungle cities
In far-off, more developed territories;
Anguilla will always be my island home
No matter how far from it I may roam.

I weep for you my country

I weep for you my country,
For the birth pains of this young democracy,
For the seismic eruption of national crime,
And the erosion of family life in recent time.

I weep for you my country,
For our lack of values and common decency,
For the loss of youth and innocence,
And our blind arrogance and self pretence.

I weep for you my country,
For our wilful ways and self complacency,
For the malicious words we hurl at each other,
To sever ties of kin and brother

I weep for you my country,
For our ruthless ways and savagery,
For crushing and suppressing our fellow man
Or trampling his dreams whenever we can

I weep for you my country
For 'this ship' adrift on life's stormy sea,
For the unknown course you have to charter,
Let's all pray, God bless Anguilla.

Dry Weather

In our island dry weather creeps in stealthily,
Shortly after the hurricane season is past;
Like a dragon it breathes out fire in the air,
Scorching all the grass and twigs that grow here;
It bakes the earth a deep dark brown
And spreads a blanket of heat over the town.

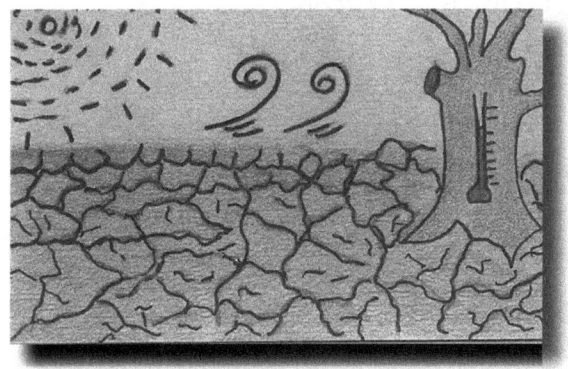

When the wind kicks up its feet in a lively jig,
Dust devils whirl and swirl across the earth's face;
Clouds of it soar high in the atmosphere,
Then float gently downwards and settle everywhere.
Dust discolours the houses that are newly built,
And carpets the floors with a layer of silt.

At the height of the dry weather's reign,

The housewife's work is never done;

From morn till night she'll find herself occupied

Sweeping, dusting, mopping; and ere the floor is dried,

Her children rush inside, dust-covered from head to toe,

And plant their dirty foot tracks across the kitchen floor.

The trees now shed their drying leaves

Exposing bare arms stretched upwards to the sky.

Leaves in the yard, beneath the trees, beside the wall,

Still the brown, rustling leaves continue to fall.

The clucking hens come scratching, searching for food

Among the leaves, to feed their hungry brood.

Soon the wells cease to yield; the ponds dry up.

The mud cracks its parched lips wide open

Waiting for a drink to quench its raging thirst.

The crops in the field so flourishing at first
Begin to droop and wither, what a dismal sight!
Ruined crops is every farmer's plight.

The dry weather season wages a fierce war
On all living creatures trying to exist here.
Neither human nor animal, tree nor flower
Can escape the harmful effects of its power.
Then nature lifts its voice in unbroken refrain,
'We need a blessing, please send us some rain!'

Folklore

Our fore-parents who came here long, long ago,
Passed on their culture by means of folklore,'
Their stories and wise, old sayings

Pregnant with subtle meanings,
Give us a snapshot of life in the days of yore.

Anguillian Politics

Tell mi wah gon wrong wid politics in dis country?

Dere was a time when one man use ti represent we.

Everybody showed him great respect and honour,

Even if dey preferred somebody else or didn't vote fi he.

Well, over de years tings gon from bad ti worse.

Today yuh gotta be careful who yuh talk politics wid,

'Cause people holdin yuh up if yuh don't support dere party,

Or dey stop speakin to yuh or shun yuh like yuh got a curse.

Everybody know that politics is a real dutty game

Some o' de seasoned politicians as well as de wannabees

Tryin ti outdo each udda diggin up any kind o' dut

To assassinate each udda's character or blacken dere name.

Sometimes our politicians behave like dem backward,

'Cause all dey do is blame one anudda fi all dat gon wrong.

Dey spend more time rantin and ravin bout trifles

Than wha dey goin do ti get dis country movin forward.

Lately there's lots o' shoo-shooing bout de buyin o' votes.

Dey say who can't gi cash givin materials or house appliances;

My vote is fi free, 'cause uh can't be bribed,

So don't try to buy mi off wid yuh hundred dollar notes.

Dis party politics dividin an alienatin all o' we.

Uh believe it's time fi we ti elect a national government;

Perhaps den we'll be lucky enuff ti get de most effective leaders

Who'll rule dis country in love, peace and prosperity

School Life

The Principal

Every child knew who was at the door
Long before he entered the corridor,
For silence preceded him down the block
Causing students to sit up and take stock
That the Principal was near.

When he strode down the hall,
No-one heard even the slightest footfall
So soft were the soles of his footwear.
He deliberately chose those so none could hear
His stealthy approach.

Silently striding along the walk-way
Which he did on any given day,
You could almost hear the proverbial penny drop
Even before he made a temporary stop
To question the class ahead.

His distinctive voice was our cue to adopt a studious look,
So we bowed low and grabbed the nearest text book;
We poured over that book's content with a fixation
That belied the animated discussion
We'd engaged in prior to his appearance.

He was always well-groomed from head to toe.
That was the figure we came to adore;
His shoes whether black or brown
Were so highly polished, that even a frown
Could be reflected in them.

Confident and light-footed, he would stride past,
Checking on the students from class to class;
He worked hard on inspiring students
Which earned him deep gratitude from parents,
Students and the wider community.

Though small of stature, he walked tall.

His imposing figure commanded respect from us all.

He wore the cloak of authority with great pride

Which encouraged and motivated those at his side

To greater heights of productivity.

A lover of learning, outstanding in Mathematics

He taught us to excel in every area including Athletics.

A strict disciplinarian, yet tempered with flexibility

He worked tirelessly to advance students of ability

Especially those who were less fortunate.

He was a true pioneer of Secondary education,

Providing outstanding service to this nation;

He will long be remembered

By the students he tutored

As a fine example of a good Principal.

My Students

My students are like chameleons

Each day they take moody swings

Sometimes they soar to mountain peaks,

Other times they plummet to the depths of nothing.

Miss Moore And The Class

As I faced my class earlier this year,

I said to the children, "Just lend me an ear."

Little Meg murmured, "Oh teacher! I fear,

If I give you mine, with what shall I hear?"

The children tittered and made a big uproar.

"Hush," I said, "the principal's at the door."

Deeply embarrassed, I faced Miss Moore

And explained what made the children shout out so.

"Children, children, you must look before you leap,"

Thundered Miss Moore in a voice so stern and deep

That little Johnny began to shiver and weep

Then timidly cried, "Please, ma'am, can I take a peep?"

"This type of behaviour I won't condone,"

Shouted Miss Moore in a furious tone;

The children sat as if turned to stone.

"I'm sorry, Miss Moore," said Maggy Malone.

"This class is out of order," stated Miss Moore,

"Teacher, I've told you so several times before,"

"Oh dear!" thought Teacher Manilow,
"Why does she hate me? I really don't know."

The boys in the class had had enough,
They couldn't tolerate anymore angry stuff,
And though Miss Moore seemed rough and tough,
Those naughty lads decided to call her bluff.

They signaled to little Johnny who sat in the back row,
To take out his pet mouse and let it go.
"Squeak, squeak," it streaked across the floor,
"A-a-a-a-ah," shrieked Miss Moore as it ran past her toe.

"Get that mouse," cried Miss Moore as she dashed in the hall,
She did not see, she did not hear the warning call.
She went crashing to the floor after stepping on a ball,
Then the children gleefully chorused, "Pride goes before a fall!"

Memories Of My Primary School Days

School days, ah, how the years have fled!
Yet fond memories linger in my head,
Sometimes they flash behind the mind's curtain,
Like fresh dewdrops on the grass by the fountain.

Now waltz with me down memory's lane;
As I sift through playground scenes of love and pain
Of naughty deeds, petty quarrels and fist fights
Or boys pitching marbles and flying kites.

The clanging bell announced the school's work day
And children jostled and hurried without further delay.
Latecomers and laggards rushed to the fore,
When they saw the headmaster at the door.

Rows of children stretched out like long ribbons
Awaiting, yet fearing the teacher's inspections;

While up and down the lines the teacher roamed,
Checking to see that each child was well groomed.

Teachers impressed on us the value of education,
So they crammed our heads with loads of preparation.
They taught us reading, writing, arithmetic and composition,
But to me, the best were grammar, poetry, and dictation.

Sometimes the class was filled with fun and laughter.
When the headmaster came, it spelled utter disaster,
For every child dreaded that leather strap
Which hissed and curled in a hand hugging wrap.

Monthly, end of term and year tests were given.
Those who aspired studied as if they were driven,
That's when the classroom became a battlefield
And competing students fought for the victor's shield.

But best of all were the school yard games,

Where children frolicked and gave each other silly names.

Skipping, rounders, hop scotch, slap-n-pinchers are a few

Of the games we played and now pass on to you.

My school days have long since passed and gone

And I oft recall friendly faces one by one,

All who played and laughed and loved together

In a bond that neither time nor distance can sever.

The Fight

Mark and Mitch were like brothers,
Best friends just like their mothers;
But something bad happened one day,
Though what it was about neither would say.

Shouts of, Fight,Fight'' floated on the air,
Faintly at first, then loud and clear.
The yellling grew to fever pitch
As children surrounded Mark and Mitch

Thwack, thump, they pummeled each other,
Bup, bup, they pounded one another,
Glaring and snarling they continued their assault,
Neither willing to make a peaceful halt.

"Hit him Mark, hit him Mitch," were the cries
Of those blood -thirsty, fight lovers urging sighs;
That's when Uncle Ben tried to part the fight,
And for his reward, received a nasty bite.

The Headmaster, attracted by the noise,
 Hastily hurried to the circle of shouting boys,
That's when he heard those thumping blows,
And saw one boy being punched on the nose.

The Headmaster grabbed each boy firmly by an arm,
Marched them to his office without further alarm,
He settled the case behind closed doors,
And what happened inside, nobody knows.

I cannot tell what the fight was about,
Or why the two best friends fell out
But one thing I know, they were miserable apart,
So a few days later they decided on a fresh start.

According to the story told by my Uncle Ben,
The two boys became staunch friends again,
And even though they are both old and gray,
Mark and Mitch are bosom friends to this day.

Life Experiences

Growing Pains

When I was growing up in Meads Bay,
My mom often quelled my youthful spirits
With a killer look which seemed to say,
You'll pay dearly for your misbehaviour.

I did not mind a spanking on my rear,
Or even a switching around my legs,
But when she talked tough, oh dear!
She caused me an inner storm of pain.

Sometimes when I really disobeyed,
I''m sure it pained her to punish me,
For she often lifted her head and prayed
That I would turn out to be all right.

There were times when mother sat me down,
And gave me a very severe tongue lashing;

I'd wriggle and squirm or even frown,
But she never guessed how bad I felt inside.

Then at nights when I reclined in bed,
Pondering on all the things I'd done,
Mom's words would echo in my head,
And flood my heart with guilt and shame.

Warning words, harsh words, no matter which,
Eroded my insides, and like an overflowing dam
Tears would stream copiously without a hitch,
Along the furrows of my scrunched up cheeks.

There were times when I refused to shed tears,
Stubbornly pretending that I just didn't care;
But deep inside where no one could see my fears,
All I really wanted was mother's unconditional love.

A Mother's Care

A long, long time ago when I was age seven or so,
I fell and hit my head on the hard wood floor,
Stars danced before my eyes,
I couldn't even rise,
Then darkness embraced me in its merciful arms.

Mother quickly snatched me up and placed me on her bed,
She really panicked, thinking I was dead,
Then I opened my eyes,
And to my great surprise,
Mom's slender frame shook with huge nerve-racking sobs.

My mother fretted and worried over me,
She gave me tablets and lots of warm bush tea,
But I tossed and turned
And moaned and groaned,
Whenever pain lanced like a knife through my head.

Mother wrapped me up snug and tight,
Then gently kissed me goodnight,
She smoothed my bed,
And rubbed my head,
To ease the tight grip pain held on my head.

Mother sat with me through the long night hours,
Then slid in beside me beneath the covers,
She hugged me tenderly,
And sang to me softly,
Until I drifted off into slumber land.

What Does Grandma Mean?

One day I heard my Grandma say to my aunts,
"Be careful, my dears, little pitchers have long ears."
The only pitcher that I knew
Was one in which Grandma put cold tea-brew,
Or kept full of fresh lemonade
Made from limes or Kool Aid.

That container certainly doesn't have long ears!
So what does Grandma mean?
Do you know?

Children are God's Gifts

Children are God's gifts to us,
Rare gems, beautiful and precious,
Gems we must care for, love and nurture
Until they shine with inner lustre.

God gave us three gems as fair as day,
Each one special in a unique way,
And I thank the Heavenly Father above,
For granting us these gifts of love.

My first child is my heart string,
Oh what joy to me her birth did bring!
I'll always have a special love for her,
For she was the first to call me Mother.

The middle child I hold close to my heart,
For his life was in the balance right at the start,
It was difficult for him and hard for me,
And I love him dearly; he's my only son you see.

The third child is the one I call my navel string,
A love string that's strong and binding,
She is the last to complete the set of three,
A gem of great price as exquisite as can be.

Yes, children are God's gifts to us,
Rare gems so beautiful and precious,
Gems that we must cultivate and nurture,
Until they are mature and filled with inner lustre.

Grandmar Can

Grandmar can do anything she sets her mind upon,
There isn't a household task she leaves undone,
Despite her age and slower pace,
She does her work with skill and grace.

Grandmar is a Jack-of all trades,
She sows, cleans and wipes window panes;
She mops the floors and mows the lawn;
Her daily routine begins at dawn.

Grandmar makes everything seem so simple,
She even irons clothes without a wrinkle,
She does puzzles and reads books without glasses,
She also walks and takes exercise classes.

Grandmar cooks better than anyone I know,
Better than Dad and Mom for sure;

Her cakes, puddings and tarts are so delicious,
But for me, everything she does is precious.

Grandmar can kiss scraped knees better,
When ever there's illness just come and fetch her,
She'll find a cure for any ailment,
She's widely known for her sound judgment.

Grandmar can make you mind your manners,
With a sharp word, a stern look or a wagging finger,
And no matter whose child you are,
You won't get spoiled by my Grandmar.

Grandmar is a giant among women,
She can compete with the strongest of men,
Some folks call her a walking encyclopedia,
Indeed she's more informative than any news media.

Brother John-The Preacher Man

The tilly lamp cast its golden light,
Shattering the deep black veil of night,
A beacon beckoning from uphill and down,
The symbol to all that Brother John was in town.

It lured the villagers from far and near,
Word spread quickly that Brother John was there,
Old folk, young folk, all poured from their houses,
Some even bringing along their unwilling spouses.

Children came milling by the dozens,
Running, laughing, holding hands with their cousins,
Skipping and shouting, they joined the merry throng
Blending their sweet voices in chorus and song.

Brother John beamed his sunniest smile,
On all who had journeyed mile upon mile,

To hear him preach the word of the Lord,
And to witness the converts he led to God.

Standing in the midst of that surging swelling crowd,
Brother John hammered his message clear and loud;
"Amen! Preach it, Brother," rang through the air,
Causing many in the crowd to shed a tear.

With pumping fist and sonorous voice,
Brother John stirred them up to sing and rejoice,
He kept them enthralled, and to his great delight,
The crowd doubled and tripled night after night.

So come one, come all, early next fall,
To hear Brother John preach near the Village Hall,
Great and miraculous blessings will abound
When Brother John, the preacher is around.

Life's Journey

As you journey along life's rugged road,
Obstacles like mountains will get in your way;
Don't be discouraged, just humbly kneel and pray,
For with Christ in the centre, all will be well.

When your problems seem so insurmountable,
Your spirit is low and you can't find inner peace,
Stop! Think! Don't slide down life's slippery slope,
Put Christ in the centre and all will be well.

When you're overcome with pain and grief,
When your back is bowed with the burdens you bear,
Cast your cares on Him, and never, never despair,
For with Christ in the centre, all will be well.

When your friends forsake you and others oppress,

When you are all alone, sick in body and weary of soul,

Reach out and seek the One who can make you whole,

For with Christ in the centre, all will be well.

You don't have to travel life's long road alone,

There's someone willing to journey with you to the end;

He is the only friend on whom you can rely

So put Christ in the centre and all will be well.

Fighting the Odds

A few years ago, you came knocking at my door,
Punched me and almost knocked me to the floor,
Dazed, puzzled and numb with fear,
I bowed my head in deep despair.

The news you delivered slugged me like a fist,
Causing my thoughts to scramble and kink in a twist,
Then came denial slyly offering me false hope,
While I groped blindly for the means to cope.

Begone, you alien! Don't inhabit my space!
What is your purpose here? My life to waste!
Like a worm, you burrowed into my fortress
Intent on causing me deep pain and distress.

Worry, anger and hurt exploded in my breast,
"Why?" I ask, "Do you put me to the test?"
No, you will not control my life!
So away with grief, doubt and strife!

Knowing that I couldn't fight this battle on my own,
I called on Him who promised never to leave me alone,
And He who created mankind gave me power
To overcome the odds. I am a survivor.

What Can You Do?

What if life's pathway is full of strife and woe?

And you don't know where to turn or where to go,

When it seems you'll be crushed 'neath a load of care,

Take heart, someone will your burden share.

If you see childhood's innocence being stripped away,

Will you say, "That's not my business," and go on your way?

Perhaps if you offered some timely advice,

You may save a young life and that will suffice.

Do you notice the crazed and needy on the street?

Do you regard them as tares among the wheat?

Mere things to be scorned, ignored or spat upon?

Objects to be locked in a place where nothing is ever done.

And what of the many deeds of impropriety

Which eat like a cancer at the fabric of our society?

Will you like the ostrich bury your head in the sand

And pretend you can't see what's happening in our land?

How can you stand aloof and full of pride?

Untouched by the plight of those whose lives are destroyed?

Now is the time to reach out and do your part,

One cheery word can bring comfort to a lonely heart.

Give of your best in whatever you do,

To help others less fortunate than you,

For it was in giving from the depths of His heart

That the Saviour our salvation bought.

Pass on God's love

When last did you stop someone and say,
"God loves you. Have a fine day."
Just think how wonderful it would be,
If you helped one person God's light to see.

When last did you tell some one you really care,
Or helped in some way God's love to share,
Every kind thought and every good deed,
Will bring comfort to someone in dire need.

Have you ever thought how a cheery smile
Could brighten one lonely heart for a while?
Are you prepared to lend a sympathetic ear
Or save some soul from utter despair?

Remember it is our Lord's command,
That we spread his word to every land,
Rise up, go forth and do your part,
To sow God's love in every heart.

Give Thanks

Come let us give thanks first of all,
To Him who made all things great and small,
For life and health and daily food,
To Him who made all things good,
We give thanks.

For strong limbs to run about and play
Healthy limbs which can move and work each day,
For every movement slow or swift,
To Him who gave every good gift,
We give thanks.

For the blessing of a truly discerning eye
To appreciate the beauty which around us lie,
For nature clothed in all its glory; the birds, the trees,
And the fresh, sweet smell of the briny breeze,

We give thanks.
For every new day we witness a sunrise,
Breathe fresh air or look at the skies,
For the early morning dew and fat rain drops
Which refresh the earth and grow our crops,
We give thanks.

For our lovely island smiling in the sun
Where we splash in the sea and have great fun,
For the happy existence we enjoy here,
And God's protecting presence ever near,
We give thanks.

The Senses

I love to hear the sound of church bells ringing,
    the sound of waves crashing on the shore,
    the pitter patter of raindrops on galvanize,
    the clear melodic tone of the steel pan,
  and the tinkling laughter of children at play.

I love to see the sight of beautiful flowers blooming,
    the sight of trees twisting and tossing in the breeze,
    the rainbow arch spanning the sky,
    the golden path the moon casts on the sea,
and the setting sun in all its brilliant splendour.

I love to smell the scent of flowers fragrantly lingering,
    the scent of fresh bread baking,
    the aroma of bush tea brewing,
    the earthy smell of fresh falling rain,
and the sweet scent of perfume permeating the air.

I love to taste the tang of home-made lemonade,
    the taste of sweet succulent mangoes,
    the taste of savoury meats, stews and pies,
    the sharp, tart taste of cheddar cheese,
and the cool soft ice-cream melting on the tongue.

I love to feel the touch of hands gentle and soothing,
> the touch of soft silk sliding on my skin,
> the smooth feel of velvet beneath my hand,
> the squishy tickle of wet sand between my toes,

and the balmy night breeze that kisses me to sleep.

A Recipe for Success

To a strong will to be the very best,

Add equal measures of purpose and determination,

Blend in lots of time and dedication,

Follow each step with care and attention,

And never, never set your dream aside or let it idly rest.

Pour in plenty toil, sweat and 'fire',

Beat out every hindrance that will your way debar,

Stir in your brightest ideas and let them draw.
Use the very best experiences gathered from afar,
Then savour the first bite of your heart's desire.

The Witching Hours

Twixt midnight and the dawn of day,
When all the world is fast asleep,
And not even one tiny creature will creep
From its hole or bed of hay;
Nature enveloped in a veil of darkness,
Sheds its wings of strife and stress.

The witching hours that herald the morn,
Are cloaked in robes as deceptive as night,
For in that time, many deeds of wrong or right
Are conceived, planned, refined and shorn.
Thus the fertile brain is at its peak,
And those who dare will use this time to seek.

Suddenly an idea comes like a thunderbolt,
And the urge to capture the moment
Is like a stampeding herd fully intent
On following the leaders in their revolt
To the end. I quickly slide from my cosy bed,
And pen the thoughts that float in my head.

With frantic haste, focused eyes and furrowed brows,
The hand journeys over the land of page,
The words take shape like rows of cabbage,
Until the whole side is filled. And I browse
Over the splattered, crossed out, untidy sheet,
To snare those vivid images ere they retreat.

In a daze, as one awaking from a bout of flu,
With fevered frame and aches and pains,
The mind stills. The energy drains.
The lax fingers forgetting what next to do
Cease from their labour with the light of morn
Let the pen drop and a story is born.

Oh! how the hours have quickly sped;
The morning sounds waken all within and without.
Chirping birds, crowing cocks and my child's shout
Are sweet music to my ears. I slowly rest my head
On folded arms and let sleep like a giant wave,
Claim my tired body in its deep dark cave.

Time

Time is a precious commodity.
How you spend it is what really counts;
Make sure it is a number one priority,
To use it wisely in very large amounts.

Spend quality time with your parents,
For time is guaranteed to no man,

Treasure the opportunities time presents
To learn from them all the best you can.

Take time to know your children,
Be their best friend no matter where they go;
Teach them well life's lesson,
All they really need to know.

They say time is a great healer,
So to those burdened by grief and agonizing pain,
Let hope and faith make you a firm believer
That in time, you will one day learn to smile again.

Take time to smell the roses too,
For life isn't all about work and no play;
Take time to appreciate the beauty around you,
And let it refresh and renew you every day.

There is no time like the present to plan ahead,
Because all of your tomorrows may never be;
Only you can decide where you'll make your bed,
Chart your course or master your own destiny.

Time will tell what you have accomplished,
When your life's work here on earth is done;
If this world is a better place when you've finished,
Yours is the victory; Life's crown you have won.

Sweet River Song

Merrily dashing along,
The river flows on its way.
Ever rolling forwards,
All the live-long day.
Rippling, rolling along,
Singing its sweet, sweet river song.

Joyfully babbling along,
The river meanders by,
Providing a living for all
Who on its resources rely,
Rippling, rolling along,
Singing its sweet, sweet river song.

Moodily tossing and twisting,
The river winds like a snake,
Uprooting trees, tumbling rocks
And carrying everything in its wake.

Rippling, rolling along,
Singing its sweet, sweet river song.

Swiftly, rushing along,
The river swings round the bend;
Swallowing acres of fertile land
When the rushing waters descend.
Rippling, rolling along,
Singing its sweet, sweet river song.

Angrily churning along,
The foaming river widens out,
Gouging deep into the earth's flesh
On its forwards route.
Rippling, rolling along,
Singing its sweet, sweet river song.

Racing and rumbling along,
The river branches to the South,
Emptying layers of silt

Enlarging the delta at its mouth.
Rippling, rolling along,
Singing its sweet, sweet river song.

The Quest

Weaving among the trees
Along a narrow trail,
Following the footsteps
Of a local tour guide.
Fleecy white clouds sailed overhead,
While the tall reeds beside the water
Tossed their heads in the fresh river breeze.

Crawling like a snail over uneven terrain,
Often slipping and sliding on the muddy track.
Tripping over treacherous tree roots,
Stepping over fallen tree limbs,
Onwards and upwards we plodded,
Despite the pouring rain.

Slowly and steadily we inched ahead,
Forging our way uphill and down,
Travelling mile after mile over marshy ground.
Sometimes treading along the river's edge,
Sometimes trampling o'er the forest's floor,
We followed eagerly, where the tour guide led.

Trudging wearily, at a tortoise's pace,
Halting every now and then to rest our weary legs;
Wondering as we pushed ahead
How much further to our journey's end.
When a tumultuous roaring split the noon-time air,
And a look of excitement beamed from every face.

Pushing around a clump of trees, at a bend in the river,
There in all its glory, we beheld the Source.
How awesome! How majestic!
Nine or more cavernous mouths, in the hilly rock wall

Spewed tons of water on the rocks below;
Thundering and roaring with all its might and power.

We gazed and gazed on this spectacular scenery
Touched by the wonder and beauty of it all;
The words of two great hymns came to mind:
'Lord, how thy wonders are displayed
Where'er I turn mine eye', and,
'Ye living waters burst, out of the rock for me.'

Romeo

It's said that Romeo was a famous lover,
Who, on meeting Juliet at a tender age,
Fell flat beneath her magical power.

He did not learn of her parentage
until he — caught in the web of love
was firmly entrapped in its sweet cage.

He thought Juliet was a gift from above
One he'd always hold dear to his heart,
His darling, his little turtle dove.

He swore that from her he'd never part,
No stupid feud, nor father nor mother
would ever keep him and Juliet apart.

But his crude way of togetherness forever
has branded him, the world's most famous lover.

Confrontation with a Masked Man

Out from the cover of the cedar tree,
Jumped a masked man, brandishing a gun,
His outstretched arm pointed straight at me.

I couldn't speak, I couldn't run;
My fearful heart beat like a kettle drum,
Transfixed by the hand holding the gun.

He demanded my purse; it held a neat sum,
All the rent money collected that day.
I threw it down, he picked it up — that bum.

I released a pent up breath as he ran away,
O what a blessing that I did not die,
In such a senseless and cruel way.

Though I'm grateful, you'll understand why
My dreams are still haunted by that masked guy.

A Personal Experience of Hurricane Donna

She came rip roaring in that Sunday night,
Rattling windows, snapping off strong door locks;
Her howling winds cackled in great delight
As they jolted the walls like aftershocks.
Lightning zig-zagged the inky skies

Frequently lighting up the box like room
In which we cowered. Soon our shrieking cries
Merged with the thunders ear splitting boom.
Bang! The roof flew off, exposing us
To the cruel force of hurricane Donna.
Like drenched kittens we remained thus,
In clinging rags that grew ever colder.
We waited for what seemed an eternity
For the storm's end, and a place of safety.

If Only

If only – two little words which return to haunt you,
Linger in the mind long after a deed is done.
They are the source of a zillion sighs and exclamations.
They tweak and shape the inner man:
Tame you into submission,
Or force you into internal warfare

Against the terrible oppressive weight
Which lies like lead on the conscience.

If only — two words which reek of regrets
For actions done wrongly, not taken or never completed;
For things said or left unsaid, they offer no solace.
They are like a pricking pin
Which makes the mind squirm like a worm.
They force the uneasy man to lie on a lumpy bed;
His tossing head to wrestle with its pillow;
And dream dreams fraught with danger
That pursue him through the night.

If only — two words which speak of squandered opportunities
Get lost in the vast sea of forgetfulness,
Or become plastered over with the bandage of time.
They are the source of countless tears
Shed over the multiple failures in our lives.

They are like a red light pointing to the promises never kept:

The plans that never came to fruition;

And the broken relationships never mended – left to late,

Then we futilely lament if only.

Election Fever

Election fever in de air,

An de candidates dun start ti prepare;

Some people start ti ketch cold an some de cough

For dere promises like viruses, an we dun had enough.

Don't talk bout de talk-shows'

Some folks usin dem ti spout rubbish thru dere nose

An de few who manage ti talk sense,

Dey blamin dem fi sittin on de fence.

A gentleman walk in mi yard de udda day,
And uh listen politely ti wha he had ti say;
I know him well fi donkey years
Yet tis de first time he in mi yard appears.

He start ti jump from one topic ti de next,
Uh know he was only doin dat as a pretext
Ti beg me and mi family ti vote for he
But first he had ti mek sure an convince me.

Den mi cousin tell mi de women tryin to tek over,
So de men dem better run fi cover,
For dey dun had dere chance and fail,
So tis time fe de women dem ti prevail.

Well uh tell her how uh please fe so
Ti see more women runnin den ever before;
Uh wish dem could form a new register
So we could elect our first woman chief minister

Now a body like mi aint no big party fan,

But uh goin try ti do wha uh can

Ti see dat dere's a good leader in de pack

Since uh don't support either de front or de back.

Uh dunno if we goin have a big upset in de next election,

But uh tellin yuh plainly, dere's lots of speculation,

Some of dem candidates aint goin ti redeem dem money

Even if they continue ti spread lies like wild honey.

Tis time we de people speak wid one voice.

Only we have de right ti mek de best choice

Of who goin rule dis country wid good governance.

Cause we don't want no more lies, confusion an connivance.

Jamaican Bus Ride

Taking a bus ride in Jamaica,

Is an experience you'll never forget,

And if you've never had the chance to ride one yet,

Just brace yourself for the swaying, lurching and stopping.

When you journey on that rollicking, roller coaster ride.

Standing by the roadside one morning,

Waiting for the bus to come that way,

Sweating profusely in the heat, so early in the day,

Time crawled by slowly as we stood there in the sun,

Waiting for a rollicking, roller coaster ride.

The small white bus swung round the bend,
And pulled up next to the group of four,
The driver got out and slammed his door,
To shepherd us into his already crowded bus
For a rollicking, roller coaster ride.

We climbed inside; there were no empty seats,
Certainly no room to accommodate four.
"Small up yuhself, mek room fe more,"
The bus driver exclaimed to one and all,
As he took us on a rollicking roller coaster ride.

Imagine our horror when he made two more stops,
We were already crammed like sardines in a tin
Yet the bus driver continued to let people in,
Cheerfully shouting, "Small up yuhself, mek room fe more,"
As he took us on a rollicking roller coaster ride.

Some were sitting, some were standing,

Some were leaning, some were squeezing,

Perfume and sweat assaulted the air.

Idle chatter and jokes flew from everywhere,

As we journeyed on that rollicking roller coaster ride.

Now if you've never experienced a Jamaican bus ride,

Don't take my word for it just put it to the test,

For when you board that bus, the driver will do his best

To ensure that you 'small up yuhself and mek room fe more,'

As you travel on his bus for a rollicking roller coaster ride.

Am I Losing It?

One day a friend of mine gave me some money

To repay a long forgotten debt that she had owed,

Please don't think that I'm trying to be funny,

But I still don't know where that money is stowed,

So I have to shake my head and wonder,
'Am I losing it'?

Oft-times I go inside to fetch something,

Yet when I get there, I haven't got a clue.

I wheel back outside deeply thinking

But nothing comes to mind of what next to do,

So I have to shake my head and wonder,

'Am I losing it'?

Once I got on the phone to call my friend,

But I couldn't remember the number I had dialed,

When my sister answered at the other end,
I stupidly said, "It wasn't you that I called,"
So I have to shake my head and wonder,
'Am I losing it'?

On my way to church one Sunday morning,
I tried to recall if I had turned off the oven,
I quickly returned home and without hesitating
Headed inside to check, but I hadn't forgotten,
So I have to shake my head and wonder,
'Am I losing it'?

One day I searched high and low for my glasses,
I really didn't know where they were laid,
I asked the children in seven of the classes;
Then a child laughingly said, "They're on your head,"
So I have to shake my head and wonder,
'Am I losing it'?

Now I have a bad habit of misplacing car keys,

So one day it happened and I didn't have the spare,

After fruitlessly searching even under the trees,

I got a lift home and left the car right there.

So I have to shake my head and wonder,

'Am I losing it'?

Last Saturday after unpacking all my shopping,

I checked to see if everything was properly stowed;

To my dismay, all the frozen things bought that morning
Were neatly placed on the shelves of the cupboard.

So I have to shake my head and wonder,

'Am I losing it'?

Here's a secret I haven't revealed to anyone before,

I lost my cell-phone and truly don't understand

How I could find it two days later in the fridge door.

All I remembered then was that I had it in my hand,

So I have to shake my head and wonder,

'Am I losing it'?

To some, such lapses may seem disturbing,

But they're common to people like you and me,

And even though this may sound trifling,

Take heed, for the time is coming as sure as can be,

When you'll shake your head and wonder,

'Am I losing it'?

Limericks

Limericks

A young lady was once heard to say,
"I'd rather stay single than wed old Jay,"
She turned down his suit,
And didn't care a hoot
That no other offer came her way.

There was a gentleman from Long Bay
Who always had just one thing to say,
When you asked his name,
Or from whence he came,
He unerringly replied, Fri-day."

A 'gal' who wished to change her last name,
Tried her luck with men she thought good game,
She dated rich guys,
Which wasn't very wise,
And that's why she's still Miss Fairgame.

There was once a young boy named Kent,
Who refused to go where he was sent,
His dad took a strap,
And beat out that crap,
After which he always willingly went

A deer and a hare planned a race
To test which one had the faster pace,
Said the deer, " I dare."
The hare didn't hear,
 So off they went on a wild goose chase.

A young man who was often in trouble,
Had a cousin exactly his double,
You couldn't tell them apart,
Yet when he was caught,
The blame still fell on poor cousin Hubble.

A classmate who was known to stutter,
Made us laugh at the things he'd utter,

The teacher for fun,
Questioned Eutson,
Just to hear him say, "Ah-don't-know-suh."

A young maid aged eighteen or nineteen,
Was terribly vain and loved to preen,
She became humbled,
Because she stumbled,
As she was presented to the Queen.

A toddler by the name of Amalgro,
Who had never spoken a word before,
Ate his grandad's food,
Which tasted very good,
Then said his first words, "Da-da wan more."

There was a fanatic young couple,
Who worked hard to stay fit and supple,
They exercised right,
But ate late at night,
So they both bulged in the middle.

End Notes

The first poem in this book, 'Anguilla, Look Where You Came From', was written for the Malliouhanna Poetry Competition on the occasion of the celebration of the 40th anniversary of the Anguilla Revolution in May 2007. Other poems submitted subsequently for the Malliouhanna Poetry Competition are: 'The Witching Hours', 'Miss Moore And The Class', 'Memories Of My Primary School Days' and 'What Can You Do?'

'A Mother's Care' and 'Growing Pains' remind me of childhood scenes with my mother and were written to express my love and appreciation for the tender care she took of us when we growing up.

'Fighting The Odds' was started after my own experience with breast cancer and was finally completed two years ago.

'Children Are God's Gifts To Us' was inspired by a sermon I heard where the preacher referred to the special love he has for each of his three children. He explained it this way: the eldest child made him a dad and was the first to call him father, the second was his only daughter and the last was his navel string.

'Sweet River Song', 'The Quest' and 'Jamaican Bus Ride' were written after visiting Jamaica and spending time with my brother who is resident there.

About the Author

Hyacinth E. Hughes was born in Meads Bay, Anguilla. She has been writing poems and skits since her teen years and later on she began writing short stories. Though none of these early writings was published, her skits and poems were used at church functions and in two of the Primary Schools where she taught. She is an avid reader. She enjoys exercising, story-telling and performing/dramatizing poems and monologues.

Hyacinth has been an educator for many years. The vast experience gained during this time has enabled her to hone her creative writing skills and is a source of inspiration for her poetry writing.

Hyacinth is married and she is the proud mother of three children.

www.ingramcontent.com/pod-product-compliance
Lightning Source LLC
Chambersburg PA
CBHW071321040426
42444CB00009B/2061